How NOT to make a Website

C.S. Rhymes

Version 2.0, 2020-01-26

Table of Contents

About This Book

There are so many books out there that are designed to tell you how to make the best website ever and that you only have to follow a few simple steps. They are normally written by people who have years of experience at the cutting edge of technology and have transformed the fortunes of some of the biggest companies in the world.

This book and this author are none of those things.

You don't have to worry about me name dropping the expanses of different companies that I have worked for and the massive achievements I have reached throughout my career. The main reason for this is that I have only worked for a few different companies and I have not yet attained any massive achievements.

What I have learnt from over twelve years' experience of working on websites is that there are many things to avoid when making your website, in a sense, I have learnt How NOT to make a website. I want you to succeed by sharing my knowledge and experience to help you avoid some of the basic mistakes when creating your website, leading to a better user experience for your visitors, as well as making life easier for you by reducing unnecessary maintenance.

Although I have web development experience in PHP, HTML, CSS and JavaScript, (don't worry, that's as technical as I'm going to get), this book is not intended for developers as your knowledge probably exceeds my own at this point.

This book is aimed at newcomers to the wonderful world of websites (that's not what www stands for by the way), business owners looking to get their business online and people who may have inherited the company website as part of a reorganisation or a promotion, or even people who have been responsible for a website for a while and don't know where to start.

Starting Point

Everyone has to start somewhere and that is the most important thing you can remember. There is nothing worse than someone who pretends they know everything about the internet and making websites, when they really don't have a clue.

Imagine sitting in a meeting with someone who is continually spouting buzzwords and acronyms they have read or overheard somewhere, but without any knowledge of what they actually mean. It doesn't achieve anything and it doesn't impress the people you are having the meeting with. They may not say anything to your face, they may just be too polite to say it to you.

If you don't know about something then be honest and tell people you don't know, but explain that you WANT to know! Everyone has a different opinion and may differ from the norm but listen to peoples experiences and find out what worked and what didn't work.

As a newcomer to the web you have a great opportunity to soak up information like a sponge and make up your own ideas about what works and, more importantly, what you think will work for you in the future. The internet changes at such a great pace so the experts in the past may not be the experts in the future.

Learn as much as you can and keep learning. Once you start learning you will realise you need to keep up to date with the latest ideas and methodologies as your website can quickly go out of date and be left behind. This may make you feel even worse than when you started reading this book, but don't worry. The fact you are still reading means that you are willing to learn and develop your skills and knowledge, which will in turn, be reflected in your website.

What is your site about?

Generally you will want to make a website for a chosen subject, an organisation or a product. If you don't know what your site is to be about, but just want to make a website, then you need to reconsider if it is worth spending the effort creating the site and then the following effort to maintain and update your site.

If you don't even know what your site is for then how on earth will a visitor to your site know what it is for?

Make the website for users and NOT for yourself!

If you want to make an amazing and popular website, think about your users and what they will get out of visiting your website. This rule applies to all websites, from a hobby site about collecting toy cars, to a company website. The objective for your site can be as simple as providing contact details for your business, to a more complex objective of generating new business leads.

There are too many websites that are too concerned about looking great and having amazing flashy animations and scrolling carousels. Don't worry about all that crap. Think about what your user wants to know. If your website doesn't deliver the basic information that your users are searching for then it might as well not be there.

Think about the sites you like to use, and like to use often. I bet they are really easy to use and fulfil your needs. More importantly, think about the sites you didn't like and what is was that put you off. Make sure the same thing doesn't put your visitors off.

A user will not care about the flashy animations on your website if they cannot find what they want, such as simple things like contact details or opening hours. They will get fed up or your site after a few seconds and press the browsers back button, return to search results and then go and visit your competitor's site instead. That's the terrible thing about the internet, you only get a few seconds to create a first impression and you will rarely get a second chance.

Users generally use the internet to find information and they want that information quicker than ever. An example of this is the rise of Google, that can now provide you information on your Android phone without you even searching for it through their Google Assistant service. If you start heading towards a location you have previously searched for it can automatically provide the driving time and any traffic warnings.

I'm not saying don't care about the design of your website (we can get onto that a bit later), but think about what the purpose of your site is and keep referring back to it throughout the websites life. Create your design around the purpose of your site and not the other way around.

The purpose and objective of your site may change and evolve overtime, you just need to make sure you have it clear in your mind what the purpose is. A new business is a great example of how the purpose of the site can change as it may initially be set up to create brand awareness but over time the purpose may then be to start converting visits to online sales.

Project Management

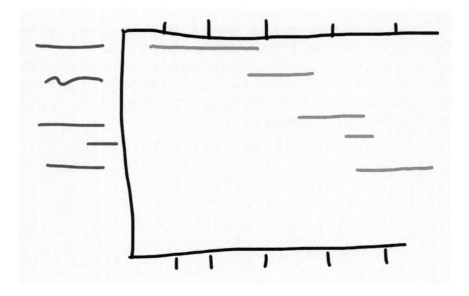

Before we start looking at what is involved in making a website, I wanted to share a bit of my experience with regard to managing website projects.

There are many different project management theories but in the real world, the most difficult part of project management is getting all of the key people (let's call them stakeholders) to give their time and commitment to a project. It's very rare that anyone is only working on one project at a time and that they can commit to a project 100% of the time.

This is where your project manager is key.

If you are a sole trader then you need to be your own project manager and ensure that you have enough time and energy to commit towards your website to make it a success. Even if you are outsourcing your website to a web development company, you need to ensure that you make yourself available to provide the information that the web developers need.

If you don't make it clear what you want and spend time discussing the options then you will probably end up with a very generic website that doesn't meet your objective. It may be difficult to juggle all of the different responsibilities of being a sole trader, but spending time on making your website a success will reward your business in future.

The same applies to a larger organisation as well. Key stakeholders need to be involved at the right time to ensure success. This can be explained further in the theory of "Stakeholder Pull".

Stakeholder Pull

Stakeholder pull is a theory I have developed to explain how the different stakeholders involved in a project can affect the outcome of a project. This theory was originally conceived from my experience of web development projects, but could also easily apply to any other type of project.

A project has a start and an end. Think about the end as the target.

The target should be what you agree the user wants and will help you meet your objective of your site. A perfect project will travel in a straight line from the start to the end.

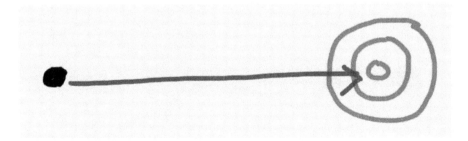

In the real world there are many different stakeholders involved in a project. This can make the line become more curved as the stakeholders pull the project in different directions. This is not necessarily a bad thing as it is useful to challenge preconceptions about what you think will most benefit the user. Hopefully, over time the project will become smoother and smoother as the different stakeholders get a better understanding of the project and all become focused on the target.

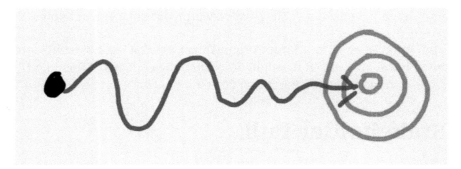

There is another potential issue with stakeholder pull which involves key stakeholders not being involved from the very beginning. The later a stakeholder becomes involved in a project, the less understanding of the project the stakeholder will have. The further along the project the stakeholder gets involved in a project, the more the pull the stakeholder has on the project. Rather than the project becoming smoother as time goes on, the project becomes more and more pulled away from the target and may end up never hitting the target.

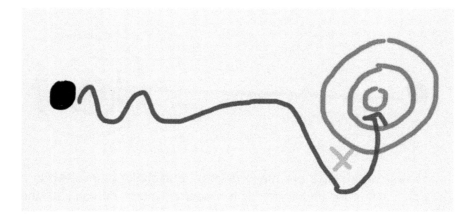

Not hitting the target means that the project has failed to meet its objective. You then have to make the decision about whether it is better to carry on putting more resources into the project to try and pull the project back towards the target, or whether it is better to stop working on the project altogether.

Sometimes, it is better to admit that the project has failed and to create a better specification next time round and restart the project, this time with the key stakeholders involved from the start to minimise the pull from the start and create a smoother project flow.

I've already got a website... Nope, that's a blog

So you have the right people involved and the time set aside to start your website project. So what is the first step?

One of the first and easiest ways to experiment with an online presence is to start a blog. There is an important distinction you need to learn in how not to make a website.

A blog is not a website, it is a blog.

This may sound obvious but let's look at what makes a blog.

A blog is a series of articles or posts about a particular subject or discussion matter, where the latest post is usually displayed first followed by older posts in a descending order.

Generally there are only the last ten posts displayed on your blog page, with older posts being archived. This means that you can't always choose the content you want to show on the page at any specific time. With a website, you can.

A blog is a great addition to a website as it can be used as a source of regularly updated content to help get subscribers and return visitors to your site, but it should not be treated as a website in its own right. You can use your blog to generate a following, but ensure that the blog has links to your main website so that your followers can then find out more information about your business.

The other thing to consider about a blog, especially free blog services like blogger or blogspot, is that they are normally on a subdomain, rather than their own domain. An example of a domain is `http://www.example.com`, whereas an example subdomain is `http://subdomain.example.com`.

This brings us onto another important aspect of websites, domain names.

Choosing a domain name

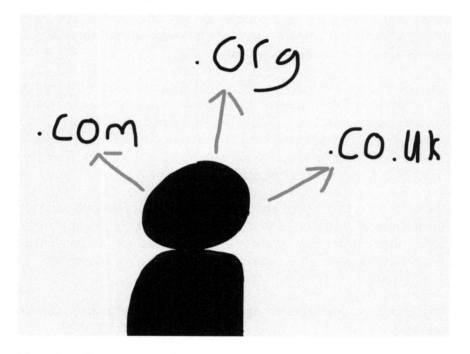

Your domain name needs to represent your brand online and is an important part of your intellectual property. If you don't yet own a domain name then you need to consider it carefully. If you have already chosen your brand name then try and get the same or as similar as possible domain name, but don't choose a domain name that is too long and try and avoid hyphens where possible.

There are so many businesses with domain names that are difficult to read when standing still looking at a poster. Consider what your domain name will look like on the back of a van traveling at 50 miles per hour. Your domain name needs to be short and sweet, unique enough to stand out and short enough to be remembered.

Your domain name (ideally as well as your business name) should relay what your business does, and if you have a local business it can also be used to state where you are based. I provided assistance for a local pub/restaurant business when choosing a domain name as they were based in a small hamlet outside of the main town. I advised them to use the name of the large town in the domain name, rather than the hamlet, as more people would have heard of the town and know that it is near the large town. Having a location in the name can also help encourage visitors to your site from search engines as they are able to establish between two similarly named businesses in different locations.

Top Level Domains

A top level domain (TLD) is the end part (or parts) of a domain name, such as .com or .co.uk. It is normally recommended to buy the domain name that best suits your location, for example, .com for USA and .co.uk for the UK. For the sake of a few pounds it is definitely worth buying both to deter someone else buying it and trying to sell it back to you at a later date.

I would avoid TLDs such as .biz and .net as although perfectly valid, they seem a bit out of date now and a .com address is much more obvious as a web address on printed material.

There are some TLDs that you should definitely stay away from as they are reserved for governments and charities. The .gov address is a prime example of government addresses, but there are also others such as .mil (short for military) and .edu (for schools and colleges, etc.).

Charities generally use the .org address as it was initially intended for not for profit organisations.

Already have a domain name?

If you already have a domain name then consider the above advice and see if the domain name fits what you are trying to achieve. Don't feel like you are stuck with a domain name forever as it is fairly easy to change to another domain name if you acquire one that is more suitable. However, changing your domain name can have a fairly serious impact on your traffic if not handled correctly. Make sure you seek an expert to run you through the risks and the benefits before doing this.

Could you imagine what would happen if Google changed their domain name over night from google.com to google-search.com and didn't correctly redirect all of their traffic? Users would try going to the old address and think that the site has gone down and revert to using another search engine.

Make sure you own your domain name

This is one of the biggest mistakes that can be made. Make sure you (or at least your business or organisation) own your domain name. NEVER let your web development company own your domain name as they will then have you over a barrel as they can turn your website off or redirect your domain name to another site without warning. I'm not saying that they will do this. I'm sure that the majority of developers would not even consider doing this, let alone threaten it. There is always the threat that a disgruntled developer may take action to "persuade" you to pay that extra invoice.

This is a worst case scenario and one that I only mention to warn you of the potential issues.

Domain names don't last forever

As well as ensuring you own your domain name, you need to remember that you don't own them forever. When you buy a domain name you normally pay for one or two year's subscription to the domain name. You get the first chance to renew the domain name but if you fail to pay the renewal fee before the expiry date then the domain name is then offered to others to purchase.

If you forget to renew the domain name then the best case scenario is that your site is still displayed for a short period of time until you pay the renewal fee.

The next best case is the site is replaced with a simple holding page from the domain name vendor until you renew it.

Worst case scenario is that it is replaced with a page full of adverts as someone else has bought the domain name and are trying to cash in on your regular traffic and the value of your domain name.

What is HTML Code?

You may be asking what code is and how the code is used in making a website. As I stated at the beginning of this book, I don't want to get too technical but I thought that it would be useful to explain a bit about the how web pages work. Generally this refers to the markup language of the web, HTML code.

Web pages are written in HTML, which is short for HyperText Markup Language. HTML is a way of marking up the content with tags to explain what the content is. An example tag is the paragraph tag. A paragraph of text is wrapped in tags, starting with an opening tag <p> and ending with a closing tag </p>. If you are interested in learning more about HTML then there are many resources, forums and code examples available online. A good starting point is the W3 Schools website, www.w3schools.com, as it breaks down each tag into its own page along with examples you can try out on the site.

Most users of the internet wouldn't even think of looking at the HTML, unless maybe you are a web developer trying to find out how the website works. Instead, you use a browser to view web pages. Examples of web browsers include Internet Explorer, Apple Safari, Google Chrome, Mozilla Firefox, etc. A browser loads the HTML and then converts the code into a format you can read and use, along with loading in the images.

The story isn't over there though. Along with the HTML there is Cascading Style Sheets, or CSS. The style sheets then tell the browser how the page should look, containing items such as the font family, colours and background colours (as well as many more things).

Another file that may be used is JavaScript.

JavaScript is a script that runs in your browser and is normally used to power the interactive parts of a page, such as an image carousel or a drop down menu.

The browser combines these three parts, (the HTML, CSS and JavaScript) and displays the final webpage to you, also known as rendering.

Hard coded pages and Content Management Systems

There are a multitude of different website management systems, as well as the good old fashioned hard coded HTML pages. When deciding on the platform for your website it may be tempting to choose the easiest and potentially quickest option of creating hard coded HTML pages.

You can hire a developer for a short amount of time to knock a few static pages together for you and then upload them to the web for you.

That's great. Your pages are now live and you can forget about them.

Unfortunately, this is not how it will be in the real world. You WILL need to make changes to your site over time, such as amending text on the page, creating new pages and removing old pages.

Make sure you can update your website!

A website should not be treated as a flyer. A flyer is created, printed, posted out and then will probably be binned after a couple of weeks. This is not how you want your website to be. You want to ensure that you can always update your website to make sure all of your contact details and offers are correct. Trust me, it will get very annoying answering the phone time after time and you having to explain that you are not doing that offer anymore or that the prices have now changed.

For many visitors to your site, it will be the first time they have seen it.

They don't know it was made two years ago and hasn't been updated since. For the other type of visitors (returning visitors) they will see little point of returning to your site as nothing will have changed since the first time they visited.

Editing Static HTML Pages

So now you understand why you need to be able to update your website, next comes the issue of actually updating your site. If we go back to the hard coded HTML pages then this will involve either you learning HTML to be able to edit the pages yourself, or again hiring a developer to make small edits to the pages, and then uploading them to the site and hope it all works as expected. This is not ideal as the more you need to update the pages, the more you will have to fork out for a developer.

Performing a small update puts both you and the developer in an awkward position when it comes to cost. You both know that a small text update should only take a few minutes, but the developer still needs to make the change, test it out and then log on to your server and replace the affected file or files. This assumes that the developer has all of the access that they need in the first place, as well as the correct file permissions. Windows based permissions as relatively straightforward but Linux permissions are a different ball game, with owners and groups for each login. There could easily end up being a chain of emails back and forth between you and the developer. Therefore, the developer will need to charge you for an hours' worth of their time at minimum.

Content Management System

Another option is to use a Content Management System (CMS). A content management system is essentially a backend to your website that you use to manage the content of your website. You can log in to the CMS and edit the pages with a more user friendly interface. The content is stored in a database, rather than being stored as text in a file. The HTML that is sent to your browser is constructed from templates and the content from the database.

This interface usually resembles a basic word processor and will often let you preview the changes before making them live. It is also easy to log back in and edit the text to fix any potential issues.

As well as editing the existing pages, a good CMS should allow you to add new pages and remove old pages. This means that you can easily create a new page to advertise a new product or service that you are offering, without the need for a developer. Adding in a new page with a CMS will also add in the links in the navigation in all of the existing pages so you won't need to go and manually edit all of your other pages so visitors can physically navigate to your new page.

The other main advantage of a CMS is that the pages will follow templates, leading to a consistent layout and display without the need for touching the raw code.

Static Site Generators

An alternative to a CMS is to use a static site generator. This is similar to a CMS where it uses templates for the page layouts, but instead of a dynamic database, the content is stored in text files and the page content is written in a simplified format called MarkDown. The site's HTML is then generated from the data files and templates and the HTML is then uploaded to the server.

Using a static site generator can be a bit more technical than logging in to a CMS, but they offer the benefit of delivering fast page loads as the HTML is already generated rather than having to be constructed from the content in the database.

Make it easy to update

The easier it is to edit your website, the more likely you are to edit the website. The more you edit the website, the more up to date it is. This means your visitors are more likely to return to your site in future to see what has changed.

As you can probably tell, I've had a lot of painful experience with editing web pages by hand and would definitely warn you against going down this route. There are so many CMS to choose from and static site generators that it just makes no sense to make HTML pages by hand anymore.

Ensure you speak to a developer about the different options for editing your site after launch and find a solution that fits your technical experience and needs.

Website Platforms

There are many different prebuilt website platforms to choose from. These are ideal for getting your first website up and running in a matter of hours, if not minutes in some cases. Some are easier to use than others and new systems are being created all the time. Below are a few of the most popular platforms that you will probably come across, but there are many others to investigate, as well as new platforms being created all the time.

WordPress

If you are looking to create your own website then chances are you will have heard of WordPress. Let me explain a little bit about WordPress and why it is so widely used.

It started off as a blogging platform but has evolved into a fully-fledged website Content Management System (CMS) that you can use to build up your websites pages as well as a blog. There are many benefits to using WordPress, including the fact it's widely supported by a large community of developers. The standard user interface is very easy to get the hang of and it is very quick and easy to create a new page and assign it its place in your sites navigation/hierarchy.

The main bonus of WordPress is that it is free to use and has many free templates and plugins to use. If you want a piece of functionality, such as social sharing buttons, then chances are someone has created a plugin for that purpose. Not all plugins are free and some are better than others.

Advice regarding Plugins

As stated earlier, a plugin is a package of code that can be installed into your website to provide additional functionality, such as social sharing buttons or an image gallery.

One thing to bear in mind is that just because there is a plugin available, it doesn't mean you should install it. In a way, it's too easy to install plugins into your site and if you are not a developer then chances are you will never even look at the code, let alone understand it. If you don't have a developer then think carefully about what plugins and templates to install into your site and make sure you test it out first on a development server (we'll come back to the need for a development server later as it's a bit more technical). Luckily there is a great WordPress community that report issues, rate plugins and leave useful reviews, but at the end of the day it's your website that will be affected and unfortunately it's your responsibility if the free plugin doesn't behave as expected.

The other issue you can have with plugins is that they are designed to perform their own job and not designed to integrate with other plugins very well. This can lead to your site increasing in size and loading time because it hasn't been as efficiently coded as possible. It can also lead to a confusing user experience when updating your site. Some plugins have their own sections in the interface which separates the functionality from where you edit the rest of the page content.

Website Builders

There are many different drag and drop website builders available, such as Wix and SquareSpace. Like WordPress, the site builders have a backend that you log into to update your site, but instead of navigating through menus you click on the page content you want to change and edit it in its final location. It is a more intuitive way of editing as you see a more realistic representation of the final page.

You can either start from scratch or use a pre-built template to build your site with. These are normally hosted with the company so that's one less thing to worry about. The quality of websites from these services is increasing all the time and are getting easier to use.

Before you start using the service, ensure you read through the pricing options carefully and see what is included in the pricing tier you choose.

One thing to consider is how much bandwidth is provided. Every time someone visits your website they will need to download the HTML, CSS and JavaScript to view the page, but they will also need to download the images and video that is on your page. The more visits you have, the more the server will push out to your visitors. This is known as bandwidth.

Another thing to consider is whether you can export your content out of the system if you ever wanted to move from the service you have chosen to another website builder service or use an alternative solution.

Jekyll

Jekyll is a static site generator rather than a CMS or a Website Builder. This means you build your pages on your computer and then upload the finished build to your server. Jekyll is a well established static site builder with a large community of users. It allows you to write your page content in markdown format and then run a script to convert your content, the markdown, into HTML.

Like WordPress, there are many themes and plugins so you can make your own website pretty quickly, the only downside is that there is an initial learning curve as you will be required to install some tools onto your computer before you get started and you will need to use the command line to run the build script.

Using the command line or command prompt may scare some users away from this tool, and that's fine as its not for everyone, but if you are a bit more technical or are eager to learn more about website development then Jekyll may be a good starting point for you.

Summary

I have mentioned only a few platforms here but I hope that it helps you to understand that different platforms offer different benefits. This goes back to the purpose and objective of your site.

You may want to start out with WordPress and this may meet your current objective, but in future the objective may change and you may have to change your platform to suit. Don't think that once you have chosen a platform you are unable to change to another, it just requires a certain amount of skills, time and effort to change.

Website Design

This is such a large field to cover and could be a whole series of books in its own right! Instead of trying to cover everything, I'll try and point out some of the basics of web design and the items to try and avoid.

Where to start

Firstly, as stated previously, you need to understand what the purpose and objective of your site is. Once you have your objective you then need to build this objective into your design. This sounds easy, but is actually very difficult.

If you run your website for yourself and by yourself only, then you are actually quite lucky at this stage. It means that you have to do all of the work yourself, but it also means that you don't have to spend hours in meetings discussing every detail or trying to convince others that your ideas are the best. Many company websites try and accomplish many different objectives set by each part of the business. This can lead to a lot of competition between stakeholders, rather than creating a collaborative atmosphere.

This is why it's so important to have a defined objective, as you can then discard any suggestions that do not meet the objective to ensure the site stays focused. If everyone involved understands what the objective is then once the initial discussions are out of the way everyone can get on with making the site a success.

Designing on Paper

There is a tendency for people to go straight to their computer and open a graphics program when designing a website. There are many issues with this, including the time involved, but the main issue is that it is often a solitary process where the designer mocks up some ideas, they get discussed in a meeting and then the designer has to make some amends. There is a potential for this to turn into a never ending cycle of amendments.

Instead, break this cycle by getting the key stakeholders involved straight away. The key stakeholders should not only be senior managers, but the web developers and web designers so they can hear the comments first hand. It seems crazy to me how developers and designers have to interpret meeting notes or comments passed on down through the chain like Chinese whispers.

Remember that your developers and designers are not mind readers. The more you include them at each phase, the more they will understand the reasoning behind decisions and why they have been made. They can offer advice from their own experience of what works well and what to avoid.

Create a list of the elements that are needed by each part of the business and then rank them according to how well they meet your objective. Try not to say that one element is more important than another as this could cause even more discussion (or potentially arguments), instead only refer to the objective of your site as the most important aspect.

Once you have a list of your elements and their ranking try drawing the elements onto a landscape piece of A4 paper with the highest ranking element being the most prominent. At this stage of the design phase don't worry about the colour theme and style, just worry about how the elements of the page should fit together. Give yourselves up to an hour for this task and see where you get too.

If I'm honest, I don't expect you to be able to produce a working design that you all agree on. If you have, then that's great, but the point of this exercise is to demonstrate the difficulty that a web designer has to manage with the many different sections of your organisation bidding for the prime real estate of your homepage. This is why it's so important to provide your web designer with a clear objective to get the results you really want.

Once equipped with these sketches and feedback, the designer and the developer have a much better understanding of what you want, and therefore, what to do. Spending time getting a better understanding at this phase will make the following design phases easier.

Mock Ups or Prototypes

The next decision is a very important one. Traditionally, the next phase would be to create a load of image mock ups that are used to explain every possible scenario and event. This can be really time consuming and lead into a never ending circle of questions and new screen shots being created to explain what happens. After a while you end up with a monster Photoshop file that contains so many images and layers that you start to lose understanding of what each one is supposed to represent.

There is an alternative to this mayhem.

Get your designer and developer to work together to create a prototype. Yes, get them to work together, rather than independently. They can then discuss each other's ideas as the prototype is being created and takes form. The prototype should contain the basic functionality of the site and a basic design theme.

You can either wait for the prototype to be at a fairly complete phase before presenting back to the stakeholders or you can get them involved after each part of functionality is created in the prototype. Each has its benefits and drawbacks. Presenting the complete (or as complete as a prototype can be) prototype allows the stakeholders to get a better understanding of the whole, but presenting each element individually allows the feedback to be focused on that element and generating more specific feedback. The individual elements can then be tweaked before the whole is presented.

Involving stakeholders more regularly also helps them to feel included in the overall process and helps get more regular communication.

Once the functional prototype has been presented and agreed, more time can then be spent by the designer and developer smartening up the final design. They now know exactly what needs to be included and what it needs to do.

Whitespace

Whitespace or negative space is an important part of design. It is tempting to fill every last space of your site with buttons or information, but it can be really distracting. To combat this and let your site appear less cluttered and clean, try deliberately leaving space around key elements. Weirdly, the negative space actually makes it stand out more.

Think about the websites you really like to use and that look clean and modern. I bet they have areas of whitespace around elements of the page. There is definitely a careful balance between too much clutter and too much whitespace as you still want to ensure the key information and actions are present, but if users cannot distinguish the key actions from other parts of the page then they might as well not be there.

Writing Content

There are lots of rules about writing content for print. Once something is printed, it is physically printed and cannot be edited. The same does not apply to a website where you can change the content as and when you please. However, this doesn't mean that you can get away with poorly written or misleading text on your website.

The content of your website reflects your business or organisation, so if there are mistakes then this will reflect badly on you or your company. Therefore, double check it or, even better, get someone else to check it over as well before making the content live on your site.

There are some important considerations when writing content for the web as opposed to traditional printed material.

Informal Text Style

The thing to remember about the internet is that it doesn't necessarily follow the same rules as standard text. The text in many sites is written in an informal style to appear more personalised and make the visitors feel more at home. The last thing you want to do is appear too corporate or like a faceless machine (unless of course this is what you are looking for in your website). You want to represent your company as the friendly and customer focused business that it is (or at least that I hope it is).

Here are a couple of examples to help demonstrate what I mean:

- Welcome to our online store. We sell product X and you can buy it from us here

- Hi there! Welcome to our online store. Feel free to check out what we offer, including product X, our best seller

Example a) is very formal and to the point but it doesn't really make a visitor feel like they are establishing a connection between them and the online store.

Example b) is informal, leading to a much better impression by being a lot more friendly and welcoming. Try and consider writing text as a conversation.

If you have a login on your site, you can improve example b even more by adding in the visitors name into the text. This is personalising the site to your visitor which is exactly what you would do for a regular visitor to your real world shop. You need to be careful that you don't go too far with this attempt at personalisation as it can soon become a bit creepy.

For example Hi there Dave. Welcome back to our online store. Its been 16 days and 14 hours since you last visited. We have more of product X ready and waiting for you

See what I mean! Personalise but don't take it too far.

Large Blocks of Text

You may feel really passionate about your products or services and want to write an essay about how good your business is and how it is so much better than your competitors, but don't put it on your website as no one will read it.

When using a website, people don't want to read through a large block of text to get answers, they want you to tell them the answer as quickly and easily as possible. Text is important on a page, but if you can provide the information in a more visual way, such as through a picture, then the user will be able to digest the information much quicker. Whatever your site is about, make sure that you have pictures so that visitors can understand what your page is about at a glance as they may not spend more than a few seconds looking at the page.

Headings & Subheadings

If your site is very text focused, then ensure that you include relevant headings and subheadings. Headings have been part of webpages for a very long time and are supported in all major browsers, but they are often misused or even completely missing from pages.

Headings are used to help break up the page and allow a visitor to see what each section of text is about without reading all of it. This allows users to pick and choose which content they feel is most relevant to them and read that first.

Headings go from heading one (<h1></h1>) down to heading six (<h6></h6>) and should be used in ascending order (starting at h1 upwards).

Consider how a newspaper headings are used in the printed pages.

The largest heading is the stories headline. This is like the heading one on a webpage, explaining what the page is about. The story might be quite long and discuss slightly different aspects of the story.

To help break up the story into chunks a subheading can be used. This is like the heading two tags on a web page.

Headings can also be nested, so if you have two heading twos on the page then each can have multiple heading threes under it to further break up the text. For example:

```
<h1>heading one</h1>
<h2>heading 2</h2>
<h3>heading 3</h3>
<h3>heading 3</h3>

<h2>heading 2</h2>
<h3>heading 3</h3>
<h3>heading 3</h3>
```

You should also note that each page should only normally have one "heading one" (or <h1>) tag. The heading one tag should describe what the whole page is about, whereas the rest of the headings describe the sections of the page. This is a basic rule for your pages. If you feel that you need a second heading one on the page then the second section of content should be moved into its own page as it's too different from the first section of the page.

People Don't Scroll

I don't know where this misconception came from but everyone scrolls webpages. If someone tells you that all of the content of the page needs to be above the fold then simply reply to them "Tell me what the fold is". This will throw them off and they will probably reply that "The fold is what you can see on the page when it loads".

You can either leave it there and smile smugly at yourself knowing that they don't have a clue what they are talking about or you can take the opportunity to point out to them that most devices have different screen resolutions so you can never guarantee where the "fold" will be for each user. Personally I would go for the latter and then go on to point out the little scroll wheel on their mouse and then ask them what that is for. They will then reply "Well... um... er... it's for scrolling webpages".

It's true that you want to consider the order of your content and display important actions near the top of the page, but you also want to order your content in a way that encourages users to scroll the page and read further.

A great page layout will entice visitors to find out more about what you have to offer and stay on your site. One way of encouraging scrolling is a well-placed image that visitors can only see part of and want to scroll down to see more of.

Moving From a Text Document to a Web Page

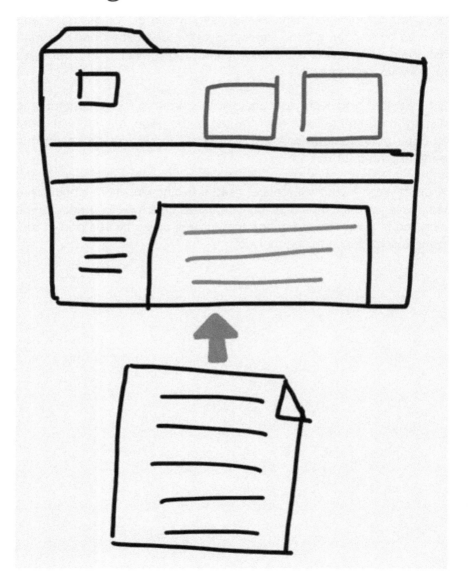

So now you have written your content there are some considerations for how you get that text from a word processor into a web page. Text will look different on different screens and different devices so try not to get too hung up on making it wrap exactly, as you cannot guarantee the way it will look to your user as you can't tell if they are using a desktop, laptop, tablet or smartphone.

Spell Check But Be Wary of Text Editors

This may be a really simple suggestion but make sure you run your text through a spell check and a grammar check. This is one of the easiest ways of removing potential typos from your text before adding it to your site. It is always recommended to get the text worded correctly before you put it on the page but sometimes it may not look quite right when it is on the page.

Be wary of copying text from a word processor, such as Word, as it may inadvertently copy some additional formatting into the end web page. If you have styled your text in your word processing software then certain browsers may try and emulate this style by adding in HTML tags by itself to make things easier for you. This can cause issues as the code will not be as clean and correctly formatted as you would like and could cause issues when you come to edit the page at a later date. This issue can still occur on web based text editors as different browsers behave differently.

To avoid these issues, copy and paste the text from your word processing software into a plain text editor, such as Notepad, and then copy it from Notepad and paste it into your site. The intermediary step ensures that only the text itself is copied and no additional tags will be created.

Another issue I have experienced is that sometimes characters such as hyphens and apostrophes are replaced with random characters and do not get rendered correctly in the final webpage. This can sometimes be due to the different fonts that are used in different packages. I've also seen text in certain file formats, such as PDF, having additional line breaks and extra spaces in words so be extra careful when copying from this format.

Markdown

Another way of ensuring that the text you have entered is rendered correctly and is clean from unwanted tags is to use Markdown.

Markdown is a very simplistic formatting method that is also quite powerful and is very quick to learn. The idea is that you create all of your content in Markdown format and then the site converts this content into HTML when it renders the webpage. This is not always possible with all websites but check if your site is capable of accepting text in markdown format as it is becoming very widely used.

An example of Markdown format is to use a hash to signify a heading one, two hashes for a heading two and so on.

```
# Heading 1
## Heading 2
```

As stated, it's quite easy to learn the basics. For more information on Markdown and the formatting visit https://daringfireball.net/projects/markdown/

Images

The internet would be a very boring place without images. When the internet started it was purely text based as it reflected the technology at the time, but now we don't have that problem.

Quality of images

Whatever your site is about, the better the images, the better the impression of the visitor will be. As discussed previously, visitors may only spend a few seconds on your website before pressing the back button to go back to search results. A great image can be used to grab a visitor's attention and make them read more of your site.

If you are using your website to showcase your product offering then invest in high quality photography. A camera on a smartphone may be good enough for taking a selfie to post on Facebook, but they are not good enough for a website. The issue may not be the resolution of the image (many camera phones have 8 Mega Pixel + cameras) but the quality of the lens and the correct lighting from a professional photographer can make such a massive difference.

I'm not saying you need to upload these super high quality images, as many images on the internet are compressed, but if you compress an average picture it will look a lot worse that when you compress a great picture.

If you are unable to get the high quality images for your site then consider purchasing stock images from another site or ask your suppliers for high quality images of your products. I'm sure a supplier will be willing to help, especially as it may help them sell more of their products.

Text in Images

Just don't.

As you can't guarantee what screen size will be used to view your site, avoid embedding text in images wherever possible. The image may seem fine on a large desktop display, but the same image on a smartphone will be a couple of inches across and the text can become unreadable.

Unlike images, text in HTML is scalable to any size and can be adjusted through style sheets to suit the screen size and device resolution. A good developer should be able to make the image a background image with text over the top.

Screen Size and Resolution

The biggest problem we have with images now is the massive differences in screen sizes. A visitor to your site could be using a 30" monitor, a 15" laptop, a 10" tablet, a 7" tablet or even a 4" smartphone screen. What makes it even worse is that some smartphones, have the same resolution as a full HD TV but a fraction of the size.

This leads to a dilemma with images. Do you upload a ridiculously large image that is suitable for a really high resolution screen, but takes ages to download, or do you upload a low resolution image and hope it looks ok?

Weirdly I don't think there is an absolute answer to this question yet. One option that works well is to load a lower resolution image as a placeholder so the user can use the page (without the page layout moving around when the image loads in) and then load in a higher quality image over the top once its downloaded.

Another option is to load in an image that is twice the resolution you need, but is more highly compressed. The page will then resize the image to fit and should look good on both large and small displays.

A more technical option is to look at the image format you are using. If you want a compressed image then go for a jpg image, if you need an image that is partially transparent then go for a png, but if you want an image that looks good at any size then consider an SVG.

SVG stands for scalable vector graphic. These are images that can be built in a certain way and represented in a form of code, allowing them to be scaled to any size. These are a more specialist image format but a professional designer should have an understanding of how to create them. Anyway, apologies if that got a bit technical, I just find it interesting.

Search Engine Optimisation

Working on a website will probably lead you to start receiving phone calls and emails from Search Engine Optimisation (SEO) agencies. They will claim that they can get you to the top of Google for a particular search term for a particular cost and something along the lines of "we are the best thing since sliced bread".

Hopefully you will understand from the tone of this paragraph that I am very wary of SEO agencies. If you are interested in seeing what a search agency can do, then look at what they have done for their other customers and don't jump straight into a long term contract as you want to ensure you have some flexibility if you don't feel it's working out as expected.

Link Building

There is no magic bullet to getting your site to the top of a search engine, it takes time and energy. Search engines use links as a measure of your sites popularity but they also weigh the importance of the sites the links come from. There are some easy ways to get links to your site but they will probably be really awful sites that exist just to contain links, which can actually end up damaging your ranking rather than improving it.

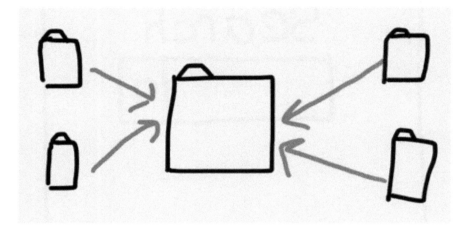

So what should you do to get links? Make your site great and worth linking to. If we go back to the earlier example of a website for a toy car collector then you want to make your site the authority on the matter of toy cars by having the best quality text content, images and regularly updated articles. This will then encourage your visitors to link to your site from their sites and blogs and reference your site.

Like I said earlier, it takes time and effort!

Blogging

If you are keen on writing then write regular blog posts about your site's subject to help build up additional content for regular visitors to read. These blog posts also help search engines understand what your site is about and can help increase your ranking for specific terms. Taking the earlier example of a toy car site, write blog posts about specific toy cars and what makes them stand out, but then also ensure to link back to the specific product you are discussing. This makes it easier for your visitors to go to the product page, but also associates the content with the product in the eyes of search engines.

Link Text

If you have a link in your site then try and make the link text descriptive and avoid using 'click here' as the link text. It's much better to have a link that says 'Toy Cars for sale' than 'click here' for search engines but more importantly for your visitors too.

Meta Data

Another important aspect of SEO is meta data. Meta data is content that is read by search engines to help them understand what your site is about. There are three basic items to consider; page title, description and the URL itself.

Page Title

The page title is normally used by search engines as the link to your site and is the most prominent part of the search result. There are many sites that just have the page title for the sites homepage set as "Homepage". This tells the search engine nothing about what your site is about. Use page titles to describe exactly what each page is about, but concisely. Search engines will generally not display more than 50 characters for your page title.

Description

The description is normally used for the snippet underneath the page title in search engines. Again this should be used to describe the page, but in a little more detail. You still only get around 150 characters displayed but this gives you a chance to really sell your site and encourage users to click through. Don't be tempted to fill up the description with a load of keywords to try and increase its ranking. The description needs to be clearly readable otherwise it will put people off from visiting your site.

URL

The URL is something that people quite often forget about. A lot of CMS have automated URL generating systems based on an automatic ID of the page that has been created. An example of this is www.example.com/?articleid=1234 which looks pretty awful. Instead, look for options to use more search engine friendly URLs that contain the hierarchy of the site and the page title to make the URL. An example of a more search engine friendly URL is www.example.com/article-category/page-title/ . This URL gives search engines an understanding of what the article is about and where it belongs within your site, allowing it to better classify your page.

Search Engine Webmaster Tools

The major search engines offer their own set of webmaster tools that can be used to help you understand how the search engines see you site and what terms you rank for. They also offer guidelines to help you improve your rankings, including listing out pages with missing or duplicate page titles, pages with short descriptions and much more.

To help search engines find all of your pages it is important to create a sitemap file. The sitemap is written in a specific format that search engines can read. Many website platforms offer a sitemap by default or a plugin to generate one. Once you have generated your sitemap, log into the search engine webmaster tools and submit your sitemap to it. The search engine will then check back at regular intervals to find new pages.

I will not go into this in any more detail as each search engine provides different tools. Just make sure that your web developers are aware of these free tools and read the search engines guidelines to give your site the best chance of ranking.

Backups, Development Environments and Staging Environments

This is one of the parts that is most often forgotten until it's too late. Many people make their site locally on a single computer before copying it over to their hosting server and then forget about it.

Developing on a single computer in itself is a risk as there is potential for work to be lost before the site is moved to the server. If something happens to your site or the server then there is potential for you to lose part of your site or even your entire site.

To help prevent this from happening you need to make sure there are multiple copies of your site in various locations. This might sound like a bit of overkill for a simple website with a few pages, but it will save you a lot of effort in future.

If we go back to the original issue of developing on a single computer, there are many online services, some free and some at a small cost, that provide hosted version control for your code. Version control allows you to save (or commit) your code changes as you go along and ensure you have a backup of the code in another location. This means that the developer can commit their changes each day and if worst comes to worst, they can then pull the most recent version of their code to another computer and carry on where they left off.

You can take version control one step further and use services like GIT (yes, that's the real name for it), that allows multiple developers to work on one system at once. GIT allows you to create branches of code so developers can make their changes and test them before merging the changes back in to the main branch (master branch) of the code.

Spending a little time understanding and refining the development process before the development starts will make the process a lot easier in future, as well as reducing risk of losing work.

Version control is usually only for the code base and does not include other parts of your site, such as the database and image files. Therefore, ensure you back up these separately. If your hosting company offers a backup service then definitely look into it, but always have your own back up locally, and more importantly, making sure the backup is always up to date! There is little point in having an out of date backup.

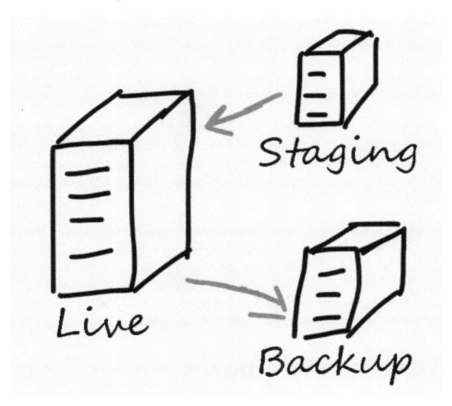

Development Environment

I will try and explain why it is important to get the development environment sorted without getting too technical. The development environment is the developers own version of your site under their total control that they can use to build new pages and new functionality. Hopefully your developers will be clued up on this already and you won't need this advice, but it is always useful to have a basic understanding of what your developers need.

There is often a choice between hosting your site on servers running either Windows or Linux. There are many different versions of Linux to choose from as well. Whatever operating system is chosen, make sure that your developers are able to emulate and develop on exactly the same version of the operating system. This applies to all of the versions of software running on the server.

This may seem like overkill, but when it comes to pushing something to the hosting server you can never be 100% confident it will work as expected if it isn't fully tested on the same configuration somewhere else first. Again, getting this right in the beginning will save you time later.

Setting up the development environment doesn't necessarily mean purchasing a load of additional hardware as there is the option of setting up a virtual machine on an existing computer that will run a different operating system and configuration. This can be quite a demand on the computer, so make sure that your developers have high specification computers to be able to do this.

Staging Environment

As well as having somewhere set up for your developer to work and test, you will also need somewhere for your developers to show you their work in situ, like a dummy version of the site. This is known as a staging environment. This allows you to have a look at how a new page or piece of functionality will work without affecting the live website. This should not be used as a place for bug testing, only looking at finalised code. Like the development environment, it should also be based on exactly the same configuration as the hosting server.

The staging server should be locked down with a username and password so that only permitted users can see it, as well as preventing search engines from finding it and risking the staging version being listed on search engine results.

I'll say it again, getting this infrastructure in place may seem over the top but it will help make the process flow of development, testing and previewing changes before making them live a lot smoother.

Testing

Over the last few chapters I have touched on the need for testing, but I feel it's so important that it needed its own chapter.

The developers should be responsible for the technical aspect of testing and ensuring the functionality works as expected, but as a stakeholder of the website you should also be involved in testing. This is so you have a better understanding of your website and how it works as well as giving you ideas and inspiration for how you can keep making your site better.

If your site has multiple stakeholders then it's important to get them to test as well. This is sometimes known as user acceptance testing (or UAT) and is useful in proving that you have met your objectives.

As stated in previous chapters, you cannot tell what device someone will be using to view your site so make sure you test your site on multiple devices (and in multiple browsers at that matter) to get a better understanding of how your site behaves on different screen sizes. You cannot simply test on a desktop computer anymore as more and more users are using tablets and smartphones to browse the internet. If anything, maybe you should start with the smartphone and work up from there. If it works great on a smartphone then there is a good chance it will work well on a tablet too. Make sure you test your site both in portrait and landscape modes on tablets and mobiles.

Using a touch interface is very different from using a keyboard and mouse. You can be a lot more precise with a mouse than you can with a finger or thumb. Don't just assume that the website will work on a tablet because it's fine to use on a computer.

Other considerations include the fact that a touchscreen device has an onscreen keyboard that covers a large part of the screen when active. Therefore users may only be able to see the text box they have clicked on and not see other parts of the screen that may contain instructions.

Testing on devices might seem like an expensive outlay at first but once you have the devices, I'm sure that you will find other uses for them, such as using your email or quickly checking and updating your company's social media presence. I have found the WordPress app (if you decide to use the WordPress platform) particularly useful in the past for writing draft articles or checking and approving comments when you are out and about.

The more you test, the more ideas you will have about how you can make your website better for your users and how you can better meet your websites objectives.

Conclusion

Hopefully you will now have a greater understanding of How NOT to make a website, so that you can make your own website great. The constant theme throughout this book is to think about the purpose of your site and to let that direct your decision making. It can be really easy to get distracted from what is important and end up with a website that doesn't reach its full potential.

Think about your users, give them what you think they want, but remember that what they want and expect changes over time. The more effort you put into your website, the more your visitors will get out of it. Make it easy to update and update it often.

Good luck!

Milton Keynes UK
Ingram Content Group UK Ltd.
UKHW042059300924
1929UKWH00004B/286